11/13/83

To Stanley & Jackie!

Relax and enjoy
a good laugh at BBB our
nutty perfectionism —

Perfectly yours.

Michael Page

So ... Why Aren't You
Perfect Yet
for $4.95?

Illustrated by
SANDY BRADLEY

So . . . Why Aren't You Perfect Yet for $4.95?

The Last Self-Help Book You'll Ever Need

Michael H. Popkin, Ph.D.

With a Special Introduction by the Author's Mother

Published by
Woodbridge Press / Santa Barbara, California

Published and distributed by

Woodbridge Press Publishing Company
Post Office Box 6189
Santa Barbara, California 93160

Copyright © 1983 by Michael H. Popkin

Published simultaneously in the United States and Canada

Printed in the United States of America.

Library of Congress Cataloging in Publication Data

Popkin, Michael H.
  So—why aren't you perfect yet?

   1. Success—Anecdotes, facetiae, satire, etc.
2. Perfection (Ethics)—Anecdotes, facetia, satire, etc.
I. Title.
PN6231.S83P66 1983   818'.5402   83-16669
ISBN 0-88007-141-9 (pbk.)

Dedication

To Grandpa, Ella, and Larry . . .
the Rubin writers

Table of Contents

Special Introduction by the Author's Mother

First, I want to congratulate you for being so smart to buy my son, Michael's, book. He worked very hard on it, I'm sure, and if Michael wrote it, it must be very, very good.

After all, Michael always did his best. That's all we ever asked, that he do his best. Like the day he brought home all A's except for a "B" in English, and I looked him in the eye and said, "My son, my son, is this your best?" And he started crying because he knew in his heart that if he had done his best, he would have made all A's.

Do you always do your best? I hope so, and I'm sure your mother hopes so too. And I hope she gives you a little push now and then, and reminds you that "practice makes perfect." I think that if a parent really loves a child, it's up to that parent to push, push, push—even after that parent passes on—as I did in 1967 . . . and I still push Michael! How do you think he got his book written? He was working very hard on a parenting education project when I jumped out from behind his bagel at Katz's Delicatessen and said, "My son, my son, are you doing your best?" He looked at the bagel funny, made a sour face, and started to cry because he knew he wasn't doing his best.

"Michael," I said, "what are you doing reading the sports page when you could be using this precious time to write a best seller?"

Never underestimate the power of a mother.

If you just bought this book, I know you'll enjoy it. If you haven't bought it yet, don't you want to become perfect? And if you are standing in a bookstore planning to read the whole thing and then leave without buying it, stop it this instant! Aren't you ashamed?

Now, if you have a friend or a spouse who *thinks* they're perfect when they're not, this book makes a very nice gift.

—*Michael's Mother*

Part I
Understanding
Perfection

Introduction

This is a book for people who care. This is a book for people who love. It is also a book for people on the road to knowledge, enlightenment, self-actualization, spiritual awareness and the self-help section of any bookstore. It is a book for people who are unafraid to confront the mysteries of life and death, friendship and love, human development and author royalties.

This is a book for people like you who have a high potential but continue to fall short of their mothers' expectations. It is a book for people who have read every self-help book written since Machiavelli, and still recognize the awful truth that they continue to be imperfect. It is for people who recognize that not only do they have an inalienable constitutional right to be perfect, but also an obligation. But most of all it is for people with $4.95 in their pocket and the companion conviction that perfection can indeed be bought cheaply.

Why You Should Be Perfect

Perfection, as I have said, is not just a right, but an obligation. Each of us bears two undeniable obligations in life. One is the Golden Rule: to do unto others as you would have them do unto you. The other is to become perfect as soon as possible, and stay that way for as long as necessary. How long is: "as long as necessary"? This varies from person to person. But at least until both parents are successfully deceased.

This, of course, hints strongly as to why you are obligated to become perfect. The simple answer is that you owe it to Mom and Dad (yours, not mine). Of course, you also owe it to Generals Patton and Eisenhower who fought to keep you free, and to Madison Avenue which has diligently shown you what perfect people own and wear. But mostly, you owe it to your parents, and particularly to the parent of the opposite sex.

After all, didn't Mom and Dad sacrifice so that you could have all the benefits they never had? And what did they ask in return? Only that you should be happy, right? Well, not exactly. What your parents *really* wanted was for you to be "only perfect"; but they were too polite to ask. So they said subtle things like "You have such a fine potential" and "Wouldn't it be great if you got *all* A's." And remember how when you were five and brought home your first picture from nursery school, your parents put it on the refrigerator? And it stayed there until you brought home a *better* one? These were polite ways of saying what they really wanted—a perfect child.

Let's face it. You let them down. Maybe they should have been clearer in their message. Would you have responded earlier if they had approached you like this?

Mother: Honey, what would you like to be when you grow up?

You: I dunno, Mommy. Maybe a fireman, or a police officer, or a doctor, or a nurse, or a . . .

Mother: That's sweet honey, you can be anything that you choose. Remember, your Daddy and I only want you to be perfect.

Father: That's right, sweetheart, just be perfect in whatever you choose to do.

Mother: You see, honey, it's not important how rich you are, or how important a job you have. All that really matters is that you are perfect.

You: Oh, I see. But what's perfect?

Father: Well, that's when you don't make *any* mistakes or have *any* flaws in your personality.

You: I see. Are you and Mommy perfect?

Mother: Not really, dear. But that's why we've seen to it that *you've* had all the advantages that we never had. So that you'll be as perfect as we'd like to be.

Father: And then your mother and I can become perfect through you. And just think, sweetheart, after you become perfect, your mother and I will love you.

Mother: And you'll have earned our acceptance.

Father: Good luck, sugar. Don't let us down.

Mother: And remember, sweetheart, we're counting on you.

Well, unfortunately, your parents weren't so direct. They *did* beat around the bush a lot. So consequently you only received their message at an unconscious level. But you *did* receive it. You know down deep how you hate it when you make a mistake or expose some flaw in your character, or can't do something perfectly the first time. You doubt it? Well, try the following test if you still aren't convinced that your secret ambition is perfection.

Perfect Test No. 1: Do You Secretly Want To Be Perfect?

Imagine yourself in this situation: You are lunching with a friend at "Billy-Bob Jenkins' Maison de Paris." You're having the cheese soufflé and marinated artichoke hearts; your friend, a mess of red beans and gravy. But this is immaterial. What is important is the question you have come to ask. Waiting for the right moment, you put down your Mason jar half filled with heavily sweetened iced tea and say, "You know, I've been wondering, what do people really think of me?"

Now here's the test. He can make only one of three possible replies. You are to select one that you would **least** like to hear:

a) *Most people think you're the greatest.*

b) *I hate to tell you, but you've got a reputation for being a real tyrant.*

c) *You're pretty mediocre.*

If you answered "c," if the very word "mediocre" sent a wave of nausea through your entire self-concept, then this book is definitely for you. Why? Because, " tyrant¹" isn't the opposite of perfect, "mediocre" is. If you couldn't be "the greatest," then perhaps you could still be a *"perfect"* tyrant (i.e., the best at being the worst). Either way, you could still pursue your secret goal of perfection. But "mediocre" to a true perfectionist is worse than a cross to a vampire, so if you chose "c," let's get on with becoming perfect. If you chose "b" or (heaven forbid) "a" as your least desired replies, why not give this book to a more ambitious person, and go back to reading mediocre books by bald-headed psychologists?

"If you meet a Buddha on the road, take the Buddha to lunch."

"Nobody's Perfect" and Other Lies

Imagine yourself in this situation: You are walking down a road in a strange land. Approaching you from a distance is a man dressed in flowing robes. The sun is radiant. Far off you hear a lark's thin song. As the man gets closer, you observe his full belly and joyous expression. You recognize this man. Was it in a dream, another life, a PTA meeting? No matter, he is within ten yards. He knows you. You know him. Then, ah ha! In a flash of enlightenment you recall his presence from Jimmy Chang's Chinese Restaurant. It is Buddah!

And there you stand, face to face with perfection. Then, remembering the instructions from a popular self-help book, you pick up a stone and kill him.

You have just wasted a perfectly good Buddah.

Why?

Because you believe that old lie, "Nobody's perfect," and if you keep smashing the brains of Buddahs, you just might become right.

If you think it takes a lot of courage to pursue perfection, you are wrong. It takes courage to *be* perfect. Any fool can safely *pursue* perfection. Nobody minds somebody who is just striving for perfection. Go ahead, strive all you want. You'll be safe. But just try *being perfect,* and watch out for some zealot from a video arcade who wants to make sure "nobody's perfect." You could easily wind up spending eternity eating moo shu pork with Buddah at Jimmy Chang's new location in the North Heaven Shopping Center.

Perfect Test No. 2: What Do You Know About Perfection?

Probably not much. If you are like most people, then you know as much about being perfect as you do about being Countess of Romanones. But don't be discouraged. After you finish taking this test, you'll know more about being perfect than the Countess of Romanones knows about being you.

T F 1. *Perfection, like beauty, is in the eye of the beholder.*

Answer: False, This is actually a trick question, because beauty isn't in the eye of the beholder any more either. With the advent of *Playboy* magazine, beauty took up residence in the eye of the camera. Now, editors from the leading sex magazines meet the first Thursday in each month over croissants and cinnamon coffee to determine

27

what will be considered beautiful for the following four weeks. Perfection, though not subjective either, is determined by a much higher authority: your mother.

T F 2. *It is impossible to be perfect if your father nursed you because your mother was already having implant surgery.*

Answer: This is *false,* because perfection has nothing to do with *anything* that happened in the past. You are not bound by your history but are free to explore every niche of your potential, unfettered by early experiences or destructive conditioning. Your father, however, was weird.

T F 3. *Perfection doesn't grow on trees.*

Answer: This is *true.* Fruit grows on trees. Perfection can only be gotten from this book, and it's gonna cost you $4.95, about the same as two dozen nectarines.

T F 4. *Most nuns are perfect.*

Answer: False. Most nuns are good people, but they are not perfect. This is also true of ex-nuns. Ex-nuns, however, are much better at the disco.

T F 5. *You can't be perfect if you have herpes.*

Answer: Fortunately, *false.* It is also false that you can't be perfect if you have hippies. It is even false that you can't be perfect if you have herpes and hippies or hippies with herpes, or the sautéed sole with lemon sauce. Later, you will learn how *any* seeming liability can be easily converted to an asset before you can say, "You'd tell me if you had herpes, wouldn't you?"

T F 6. *All Roses are perfect.*

Answer: False. My grandmother in particular.

T F 7. *Trusting in Jesus will make you perfect.*

Answer: False. Trusting in Jesus will make you a Christian. Trusting in Mohammed will make you a Moslem. Trusting in your stockbroker will make you sorry. Nothing can make you perfect except $4.95 and this book.

T F 8. *Learning how to effectively blame others will help you become perfect.*

Answer: True. Blame is a lost art. When used according to the guidelines in this book, it is one of the most powerful tools ever conceived for attaining perfection. For example, if you don't buy this book, I could accept responsibility and say that I didn't write a good enough book. But then I would cease to be perfect. So instead, I would choose to blame you by saying, "What a fool you are for passing up perfection for less than you'd pay for the tofu manicotti at "Eat Your Vegetables." More on this later.

T F   9. *Jesus was perfect.*

Answer: True. And considering his background, this wasn't easy. Jesus, in fact, was the only Jewish boy in history who actually *surpassed* his mother's expectations.

T F 10. *Anyone can become perfect.*

Answer: True. This is the fundamental truth of this book. In fact, it is easier than you have imagined, and much easier than, say, becoming an advanced racketball player.

T F 11. *Even people from New Jersey can become perfect.*

Answer: True. There is absolutely no truth in the belief that "it is easier for a camel to get into heaven than it is for someone from Newark to be perfect."

12. *When people say to you, "Oh, you think you're so perfect," it is best to respond with. . . .*

a) "How astute of you to notice."
b) "Eat your heart out, sucker."
c) A right uppercut.
d) A right uppercut followed with a karate chop to the Adam's apple.

Answer: The correct answer is "a." Though just as vicious as b, c, and d, it is far more subtle. And subtlety is a necessity for being perfect.

T F 13. *The first thing most people do after they become perfect is:*

a) Throw out their entire library of self-help books.
b) Burn their running shoes and go back to eating red meat.
c) Practice smirking in the mirror, then pay a visit to the elementary school teacher who most often told your parents that you weren't working up to your potential.

Answer: Both "a" and "b" are good answers. However "c" is the hands-down winner. In fact, a housewife from Minnesota once wrote me, after reading this book, the following letter:

"Oh, you think you're so perfect."
"How astute of you to notice."

Dear Dr. Popkin:

After reading your wonderful book, *So . . . Why Aren't You Perfect Yet? For $4.95,* the most amazing changes occurred in my life. For instance, I realized that being 5'2" tall and weighing 247 lbs. didn't mean I was imperfect, it only meant that I hadn't learned to rationalize properly. Now that I'm perfect, I enjoy visiting my third grade teacher, Mrs. Scott (who often called my parents in for conferences), and letting her know what a dumb old biddy she is.

Thank you for everything.

Sincerely,
Jenny Sue Schwartz II

14. *Being perfect means:*

a) Never having to say you're sorry.
b) You don't have to be your own best friend.
c) You can fire your therapist.
d) Your mother will be happy now.
e) All of the above.

Answer: "e." All this and much, much more can be yours when you live up to your obligation to be perfect.

The Perfection Continuum

Many people, as well as quite a few amphibians and psychologists, erroneously believe that perfection is an either/or phenomenon. In other words, *either* you *are* perfect *or* you *aren't.*

If you are one of these people, then you are probably denying your own perfection by making a variation of one of the following statements *(but your unconscious belief is really the situation):*

(a) "Who me, perfect? No way. I admit my mistakes." *(About one each July.)*

(b) "No, I don't demand perfection of myself." *(Just everybody else.)*

(c) "What do you mean, be perfect? That's crazy. All I want is to be the best I can be." *(And better than everybody else.)*

The central problem with the either/or thesis of being perfect is that it's either untrue or false. The non-central problem is that it is much too stringent. Under the either/

or ruling, none of us would ever qualify as perfect. Any of the above slight-of-mind tricks can be used to disqualify oneself from the running. Why would you want to disqualify yourself from the running? It's because a long, long time ago when Mom & Dad gave you that secret message, "All we want is for you to be perfect, dear," they said it very quietly, so only your unconscious mind could hear it.

What did they tell your conscious mind? They told it, "It isn't polite to be perfect, dear, because 'nobody's perfect' and you don't want people to think you're conceited, do you?"

So, you went underground with your unconscious orders to be perfect. Consciously, you still invoke the either/or criterion and tell the old lie, "I'm not perfect ; I admit my mistakes and shortcomings."

Sure you do. But for every mistake or shortcoming you admit, you sweep nine or ten others under the rug. Your conscious mind uses that as evidence that you are really not trying to be perfect, while your unconscious is having a heyday being 90 percent perfect.

So, here's the truth: perfectionism isn't being perfect; it isn't black or white, it's a continuum. We all are perfectionists to a degree. Every time we cringe at a mistake or fault, try to blame it away or justify it, our perfectionism is showing. Some of us have the "be perfect" message stronger than others, but we all have it.

And remember, the purpose of this book is to teach you how to realize this hidden goal which up to now you have been ashamed to admit. Go ahead, don't be just a perfectionist—be perfect! Consciously!

But before I teach you how to become perfect, let's see where you fall on the Perfect Continuum. Just how strong is your "be perfect" desire?

The Perfect Continuum

(Circle the number where you fall . . . or rise)

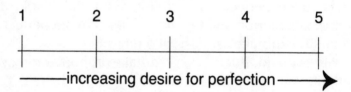

1: No desire for perfection at all. Circle "1" if you are either dead or a saint . . . or both.

2: You're basically a wimp who hasn't the guts to go for perfection except in mamby-pamby excuses that don't fool anybody. This book will make a man out of you. Unless you are a woman.

3: Like most people, you are committed to perfection but hide it from yourself, because you mistakenly believe it is a flaw to admit that you are perfect. So you operate covertly, using many of the techniques in this book, but inefficiently. (This will be the best $4.95 you ever spent.)

4: You're on the right track, aware of your superiority and accustomed to using blame and justification in a natural, flowing style to support your perfection. This book is icing on your cake.

5: Totally perfect. The last time you admitted a mistake was also the first time you admitted a mistake. You didn't like it and haven't done it since. Read this book only for laughs. You don't need it and, in fact, could have written it yourself, "If you had wanted to."

Why Hard Work Won't Make You Perfect

Hard work will make you tired. Being tired is different than being perfect. Memorize this difference.

The reason that hard work won't make you perfect is relatively complex. It would appear to the imperfect mind that working hard at something will lead to improvement. Then, once enough improvement is attained, zappo, perfection results.

The flaw in this progression lies in the "zappo." "Zappo" never led anybody to perfection—not Harpo, not Groucho, not Zeppo—so it certainly isn't going to lead you. There is just no way to leap the gap from self-improvement to perfection without some finagling. Hard work is not finagling. It is serious stuff, and as a mental health professional, I don't recommend it. For one thing, it may cause blisters. For another, I think it may be linked to certain types of schizophrenia in Canadian rats.

That notwithstanding, hardwork will enable you to attain excellence. If you're the type of half-hearted achiever who would be satisfied with excellence when with a little bit of finagling you could be *perfect,* then save yourself the $4.95 and go enroll in M.I.T. The top colleges are filled with bright young men and women who sold out for excellence. They didn't need me, and you don't either. Unless, that is, you know down deep inside of you is a perfect person struggling to get out.

The choice is yours: hard work and excellence *or* finagling and perfection.

"Not lost at all—just taking the scenic route."

Why Perfect People Never Stop To Ask Directions: or "Turn the Car Around Already"

Asking for directions is like going to confession: It isn't a mistake in itself, but it does imply that you've done something wrong. The main problem with stopping to ask directions is that you might be told that you're going the wrong way, and that you best turn around and go back to 14th St.

Bam! The moment you turn that car around, you *know*, you cease being perfect! But now for the good news: there is a loophole. If you can manage to get where you are going without actually *backtracking* then you haven't really committed a mistake, you were just taking "the scenic route." Perfect people have been known to travel hundreds of miles out of their way just to avoid "turning the car around." In fact, my research team has recently produced evidence that Magellan's circumnavigation of the globe in the 16th century was actually a "perfect" response to having inadvertently made a right rather than a left coming out of the Genoa harbor on the way to Venice.

Why Diet Books Won't Make You Perfect

Once you begin following my proven plan for becoming perfect, you will have no qualms at all about donating all 40 of your favorite diet books to the Hadassah Book Sale.

When you are perfect, the word "diet" is automatically removed from your vocabulary. The word itself smacks of imperfection, not to mention cottage cheese. To diet is to be imperfect.

Never diet. Be as corpulent as you like. Fat and perfection can be reconciled as I'll show you in a later chapter.

"But," you've been trained to say, "If I diet, I can have a perfect body." First of all, this is incorrect at an obvious level. Dieting alone will not create a perfect body. You have to also *exercise* regularly which smacks of hard work, agony, and perspiration. Dieting without exercise is a good way to create a lot of skinny flab, which is slightly more attractive than fatty flab, but not much. Then, you'll need a big hand from mother nature to get all the parts in perfect proportion.

All this and you only end up with a perfect *body*. Friend, comprehend this: we are talking about *being*

"Diet"—the word itself smacks of imperfection,
not to mention cottage cheese.

perfect, not a perfect this or a perfect that. The world is full of people with perfect *noses,* or *legs,* or perfect *derrieres,* or perfect *breasts.* There are even plenty of perfect *bodies.* But how many perfect *people* do you know?

Dieting may be good for your health, but as far as perfection goes, I recommend the Amaretto Cheesecake and all the Jamoca Almond Fudge Ice Cream you can financially afford.

Why Money Won't Make You Perfect

If money can't be expected to buy happiness, then it certainly can't be expected to buy perfection either. Unfortunately, many people mistakenly believe that when the prime rate drops low enough, they will leverage their incomes, put 5 percent down on a lifetime supply of happiness and get perfection thrown in as a premium item. Some of these same people invest in pork bellies.

Beyond the $4.95 needed to buy this book, money is totally unnecessary for achieving perfection. It is, however, necessary for achieving financial independence, a diversified stock portfolio, and selected items from the J. C. Penney catalog.

There are many good books available today that will teach you how to attract money; how to love money; how to have a satisfying long term relationship with money. These books all have one thing in common: they cost money. However, investments will be investments. So if you want to earn a lot of money, I recommend that you buy several hundred of these moneymakers, then mark them up and sell them to your friends for a smart profit. Better yet, write your own, buy yourself a grey, three-piece suit and get on the Today show.

This will make you rich, but it won't make you perfect any more than it will make you eggplant parmigiana or breakfast in bed. This is because money will only buy tangibles or services, and perfection is an intangible. Still, since there *are* a lot of tangibles and services worth purchasing, you will probably be happier being rich and perfect than poor and perfect. You'll certainly qualify for more tax benefits, and your mother will love her new condominium in the Sun Belt.

Perfect Moments
in History

28 A.D.   Jesus, upon reaching the age of thirty, emerges from obscurity and launches the most successful Perfect career in history. Perfectionists have traditionally celebrated their own 30th birthdays by engaging in massive anxiety attacks and prolonged periods of depression.

1492   Christopher Columbus mistakes the West Indies for India, effectively justifies his error and is thus given credit for discovering America.

1513   Machiavelli writes *The Prince* (originally titled, *How To Be a Despot*) and the self-help industry has its first bestseller.

1776   Thomas Jefferson writes the Declaration of Independence ". . . to form a more Perfect union," and the first society based on the concept of perfection is introduced to an unsuspecting world.

1900   Sigmund Freud discovers the "defense mechanism" rationalization—the Perfect person's favorite tool.

1914   The world goes to war, but due to superb blame-playing by international leaders, no one is held responsible.

1943   The first "mainframe computer," the Harvard Mark I, is unveiled by IBM. Unable to lie, blame, or justify its errors, the computer clearly highlights man's superiority.

1956   Bo Derek is born.

1976   Richard M. Nixon is inaugurated as our first perfect American President.

1983   Woodbridge Press publishes Dr. Michael Popkin's, *So . . . Why Aren't You Perfect Yet? For $4.95,* and unnumbered Perfection addicts proudly come out of the closet.

Dark Moments in the History of Perfection

15 million B.C. The San Andreas Fault cracks the Perfect face of California.

410 A.D. Rome is sacked by the barbarians, triggering a historical domino effect that culminates in the production of the Fiat.

1215 King John signs the Magna Carta, thus ending the Perfect social hierarchy. In a few short centuries kids will be talking back to their parents and writers demanding to be paid for their work.

1450 The first set of golf clubs is manufactured.

1564 Michelangelo dies.

Next Day Thousands of souvenir plastic Davids are sold in the Florence flea market.

1740 George Washington openly admits chopping down the cherry tree when a simple lie would have sufficed.

1937	The Hindenburg explodes and no one can think of a single excuse.
1957	The skateboard is invented.
1962	The New York Mets are granted a National League franchise.
1965	Adlerian psychiatrist Rudolf Dreikurs coins the phrase, "the courage to be *imperfect.*"
1966	The first shipment of polyester leisure suits goes on sale.
1971	The Ford Pinto.
1981	Mr. Rubik invents his damnable cube!
1983	Richard Nixon admits having lied while in office. His failure to maintain the cover-up drops him from the ranks of the Perfect.

Why Metaphysics Won't Make You Perfect

There are a lot of books around today that either fell to earth through a time warp or were dictated by a spirit on leave from an other-dimensional publishing house. These books can unquestionably change your present life (as well as your next one), but they also raise some important philosophical questions: 1) When a spiritual force dictates a popular self-help book, who gets the royalty?; 2) Can a spirit plug its book on the Donahue Show?; and 3) Why aren't metaphysics advertised in *Popular Mechanics?*

It is obviously not the intention of this book to answer such questions, although "I could if I wanted to." However, the supernatural has been drawing a lot of attention lately, and though poltergeists and witches can be fun at parties, they won't make you perfect.

Neither will taking absolute responsibility for your life. This is another popular notion that fell to earth in California, about the same time as the Mediterranean fruit fly. This false belief goes something like this: People aren't perfect; they make mistakes; when they accept responsibility for their mistakes instead of *blaming* others or *justifying* their actions, they become more perfect. The people promoting this belief also have the funny notion that they *create* everything that happens to them: for example, their parents, the sun rising over Anaheim, and, particularly, parking places. These people love to go around L.A. "creating" parking places for themselves. They never just have the good luck to "find" a parking place, they have to be willing to accept responsibility for "creating" it.

They are also, for some unknown reason, physiologically addicted to the word "absolutely." Everything is "absolutely" with them.

"Do you want to come over to my place and do some bean sprouts?"
"Absolutely."
"Are you absolutely sure?"
"Absolutely."
"Absolutely?"
"Absolutely."

If these people ever give a tentative reply, they absolutely go into absolute withdrawals and have to be detoxified in a hot tub by a team of avante guard ministers for lots of money; which if they don't have, they are expected to create.

Anyway, the main reason metaphysics won't make you perfect is because it is too busy encouraging you to become responsible. And you can't be both perfect *and* responsible at the same time. The two are mutually exclusive, so you'll have to choose (but you don't have to take responsibility for your choice). If you want a *satisfying* life, I suggest that you choose responsibility and create your own satisfaction. But if you want to be perfect (and you know you do), then it is absolutely essential that you develop your skills in the areas of blame and justification. More on this in Part II, but for now, ask yourself this: If metaphysics and responsibility are so hot, why doesn't Joan of Arc reincarnate and lead the people of California to freedom?

Why Cat Books Won't Make You Perfect

The world can be divided into two groups of people: those who love cats and those who love cat books. If you don't belong to either of these groups, don't despair; I don't either, and I'm perfect. If you belong to both of these groups . . . despair.

Statistically, the U.S. Bureau of the Census estimates that cat *book* lovers now outnumber cat lovers nine lives to one, and by the end of the decade four out of every five children will be named Garfield. Quite a coup for the feline publishers, especially considering this is supposed to be a dog-eat-dog world.

Personally, I regard cats as arrogant little fuzz balls, but I will admit this: I've never seen a cat that wasn't perfect. Seriously, ever see a cat trip over a rollerskate, or spill his milk, or make *any* mistake for that matter? No, you haven't. They're perfect, all right . . . and they know it.

But reading about cats won't make *you* perfect (in fact, it may make you laugh so hard you temporarily

"Cats are arrogant little fuzz balls."

forget that being perfect matters). I regard this phenomenon as a cat-astrophy of cat-aclysimic proportions. It's bad enough that the little fur heads have infiltrated our language as just demonstrated, but the laughter their cartoonists are generating is threatening to undermine *human* perfection itself.

So, I implore you to burn your cat books today, because if there is one thing that no red-blooded, two-legged perfectionist can tolerate, it's another perfectionist. And especially not a four-pawed, marble-eyed pile of static electricity that brags all day in soft undertones, mimicking us with its constant "purrs," which we all know is short for "purr-fect."

And besides, cats give me the creeps.

You can assert yourself, declare yourself,
transact yourself. It doesn't matter.
None of that self-help stuff is
going to make you perfect.

Why Other Self-Help Books Won't Make You Perfect

Go ahead, pull your own strings; be your own best friend; concentrate on your erroneous zones; where's it gonna get you? You can assert yourself, declare yourself, or transact yourself. It doesn't matter. None of that self-help stuff is going to make you perfect. Certainly it will make you popular at cocktail parties, and may even improve the quality of your life. But this is the only book with the ambition to teach you how to attain your secret goal: perfection.

Admit it. That's what you've always wanted—to be perfect. Every time you reach for one of those "I'm OK, let me feel you" type books, what you're secretly hoping is that *this* time you will finally make it—El Perfecto . . . The Big P.

Well, it won't work. Have you ever wondered why none of the glorious self-help recipes ever promise perfection? It's because they *know* they can't deliver. The fundamental problem is that self-help is based on the quaint notion that people can improve themselves by ingesting useful information and developing certain life skills. While this may be true, it is certainly not funny. While it may be lucrative, it is certainly not perfection. This book, therefore, which is about funny and perfection has nothing to do with self-help, and should not be expected to improve your life in any way. It will simply enable you to become perfect. Then maybe you can start sleeping at night.

Part II
The Perfect
Techniques

Introduction

Nothing worth having, not even Perfection, can be obtained without at least a little effort. However, keep your chin up, the techniques described in this section are not only Perfect, they are among the easiest skills to master this side of aerobic gardening.

I have spent years as a psychotherapist researching Perfect People and the skills they use to maintain this superior position to which they are nobly committed (often literally "committed," as the world often resents the Perfect People among us, relables them grandiose, and throws them in the funny farm). With patience and understanding, I have reduced over 1,800 of these skills and methods to six easily mastered techniques. At $4.95 for the book, that comes to less than $1.00 per technique, which is an astonishing bargain when viewed against a trillion dollar national debt, which is where *im*-perfection has gotten us.

Now, to become not merely excellent but Perfect, study carefully the following six techniques.

"Oh, I could do that if I wanted to."

Perfect Technique No. 1:

"I Could If I Wanted To"

This technique will help you avoid being asked to perform certain tasks that could be difficult and, therefore, contain a high risk of mistakes. Before the other person has a chance to ask you to "give it a try," beat him to the punch with a casual, "I could do that if I wanted to."

EXAMPLE: You are at the Olympic diving finals with a blind date. The diver, a svelte Swede has just completed an inward two-and-a-half with a full twist. Your date looks over at you expectantly, but before she can speak the awful words, you casually say, "Oh, I could do that if I wanted to," and yawn.

Your date will probably do one of three things:

a) Look impressed and say nothing more;

b) Challenge you by saying something immature like, "Well, go ahead and do it, hot shot."

c) Spill her Coke in your lap and laugh.

Response "a" of course is the most likely, but response "c" also effectively gets you off the hook as you can quickly change the subject by replying, "What do you say we go back to my place and spill some Pepsi?"

However, if she challenges you with response "b," simply switch to the second Perfect Technique, "Dodge 'Em."

Perfect Technique No. 2:

"Dodge 'Em"

The Dodge 'Em technique is designed particularly for those situations when you are asked to do something difficult. Remember, no perfect person in their right mind *ever* attempts something difficult.

This technique consists of a perfectly (what else?) constructed four-part response that has been known to make Assertiveness Training authors wet their pants with envy. These four parts are:

a) **The Setup:**
   EXAMPLE: "That looks easy."
b) **The Alibi:**
   "But I'm not in the mood."
c) **The Rain Check:**
   "Maybe another time."
d) **The Stopper:**
   "Thanks."

Each step of the "Dodge 'Em" is essential, so let's take a closer look.

The Setup. Perfect people don't just avoid mistakes where others fail, they make it look easy. Or at least *sound* easy. Above all, they never show fear. Work at developing a nonchalance toward even the most dangerous challenges. After all, you're only setting them up, you don't have to perform. Usually.

The Alibi. This is where the twist occurs, and it is imperative that you memorize at least a dozen all-purpose alibis (for sources, see Politicians and Mothers). The alibi always begins with the word *"but."* Don't let anyone tell you not to "but" them. "But" is far and away the most beautiful word in the English language, and certainly the most useful. Just lower your head, add a "t" and butt 'em right where it counts.

The Rain Check. Everybody likes a rain check, especially when they didn't have to pay for the ticket in the first place. This part of the "Dodge 'Em" response, also called "The Postponement," takes the wind right out of their sails. Usually.

The Stopper. As any Gestalt psychologist knows, the mind always seeks completion. This is why bridges go all the way to the other shoreline and brides go all the way to the altar. Usually. When you say, "Thank you," while dropping your voice with a firm and definitive tone, you effectively complete the Gestalt, thus ending the challenge. Only a Pathological Turkey would, at this point, back you into a corner by demanding that you perform.

Fifteen All-Purpose Perfect Pronouncements

1. I told you this would happen.
2. You should have let me do it.
3. What am I—a mind reader?
4. I hope you have change for a hundred dollar bill.
5. No, no, no . . . What I actually said was . . .
6. In the final analysis, all that really matters is . . .
7. Get off my planet. I mean now!
8. It's perfect! That's perfect! Perfect!
9. I don't recall having said that. Are you sure . . .
10. Oh, yes, I was just about to do that.
11. I know I seem harsh, but I just expect a lot from you.
12. Don't let it happen again.
13. You're fired.
14. You're fired, you idiot!
15. Oh, don't be so sensitive.

What To Do When Backed Into a Corner by a Pathological Turkey

Pathological Turkeys are the natural enemies of Perfect People. These beady-eyed little vermin stalk the earth relentlessly, searching for their better halves, the Perfect Persons they would not become. Each time a person becomes perfect, two things happen: 1) the profits on self-help books drop, and 2) an ordinary turkey becomes pathological.

Turkeys, as you know, are always in abundance. But inasmuch as they are quite harmless, at times even amusing, there is generally no need for concern. However, by some strange synchronicity of the universe, at the very moment one person accepts his obligation to become perfect, one of these turkeys (they have shirked *their* obligation) completely freaks out, becoming pathological and sticking large portions of cranberry sauce up their nostrils. This now-Pathological Turkey (who, by the way, is often a younger sibling of the Perfectionist) lives with one goal on its rotten little cranberry-stained mind: To prove that "nobody's perfect." At night, if you listen closely, you can hear them down by the river chanting in an effeminate falsetto, "Nobody's perfect; nobody's perfect."

What To Do

So what do you do when backed into a corner by one of these obnoxious little creatures who demand defiantly, "If you're so perfect, why don't *you* try it." (What they mean, of course, is, "Try it and fail," thus proving their idiotic thesis that "nobody's perfect.") So here's what to do:

Perfect Technique No. 3:

Attack and Distract

The best defence is often a good offense, and Perfect People can be some of the most offensive people in the world. The strategy in the A & D technique is to distract the challenger from his demand by refocusing the conversation on one of *his* deficits. This technique is particularly effective with Pathological Turkeys, because: 1) they have so many flaws to attack, and 2) they are so insecure they react with knee-jerk defensiveness to almost any attack.

For Example:

When your date says, "OK. If you're so hot, go ahead and try it"—why not respond with one of these handy A & D replies?

a) Excuse me, but I couldn't help noticing that your nose is extending into my air space. How many kilos is that thing anyway?

b) You know, there is a difference between being assertive and being aggressive. Your last comment suggests to me that you still have a problem handling the very heavy burden of rage you carry. Let me give you the name of a very good psychotherapist.

c) Have you had a bad day? Or is hostility your usual style?

d) I just noticed that when you get angry you get these two awful looking vertical lines above the bridge of your nose and your nostrils flare in a way that makes you look like a bull gorilla on the make.

e) Let me ask you a question. When you were a child did your mother ever yell at you and say, "When you grow up, I hope you have a child as bad as you!"? I bet you really caused her some grief, didn't you?

f) I'm sorry. What did you say? I guess I got distracted wondering how such an intelligent person as you could put clothes together in such comical combinations. Either you plan on taking me trick-or-treating later or you've just finished reading *Dress for Distress*.

Sidestepping the Turkey Traps

Here are some things Pathological Turkeys will attempt to do to you in trying to prove their point, and what you can do about it:

1) Often they will suggest that you attempt challenges of heroic proportions, such as performing colostomy surgery with only copper tubing and a monkey wrench. Then when you screw up, they can sympathetically say, "Oh, well, nobody's perfect."

What To Do?

This is a good time to lie. Cop a hyper-sincere expression, lower your jaw and say, "Oh, I did that last year, and frankly, it was surprisingly dull."

2) They like to send you self-help books instead of real presents on your birthday. The intent here is to subtly imply that you still *need* improvement. Accepting such a gift, by the way, constitutes tacit agreement, and can be held legally binding in certain parts of Afghanistan and Poland.

They like to send you self-help books instead of
real presents on your birthday.

What To Do?

Return this book-trap immediately with your version of the following note:

Dear Anita,

Thank you for your thoughtful gift, *Thirty Days to a Fuller Bosom*. I am sending it back to you as I am afraid that it would just gather dust on my shelf while I was out on one of my frequent dates.

When I realized this waste, I said to myself, "Self, who could *really* use this book?" Then I thought of you. Since I know you're the type of person who gives a gift that *they* would like to receive, I knew you'd appreciate it. By the way, I'm also sending you a copy of the just-released *Are Your Buns Becoming You?* Enjoy.

Sincerely,
Jeannie

3) Many of these P.T.'s become managers. If you inadvertently find yourself working under one of these snively little twirps, he will in all likelihood call you in for "little chats." During such times he will attempt to point out little imperfections, such as, say, embezzling $200,000 in corporate funds or growing a marijuana crop in your locker.

What To Do?

Listen politely, neither agreeing nor disagreeing. Nod your head from time to time indicating that you are hearing him out. Act interested, even concerned. When the monologue is concluded, ask if there is anything else. Again listen intently. When you are sure you have heard it all, then—and only then—get up and clip your fingernails on his desk. Perfect people do not work for Pathological Turkeys.

14 Things Perfect People Never Say

1. I'm sorry.
2. My mistake.
3. Oops, I goofed.
4. I forgot.
5. Please. (Except when used sarcastically.)
6. I see your point.
7. Help! My head's stuck!
8. I changed my mind.
9. Which way is it to *anywhere?*
10. I could be wrong.
11. Oh my God! I left the lights on!
12. Have you seen my galoshes anywhere?
13. Excuse me, where is the nearest bathroom? (Perfect people appear not to need such facilities.)
14. How was it for you? (Perfect people don't really care how it was for you.)

Perfect Technique No. 4:

"Blame"

Blame, as a technique for preserving perfection, is without parallel. (True, it doesn't actually intersect anything either, but this is a matter to cover in one of my more mathematical essays.)

Blame is a thing of beauty. When applied properly, it lilts with a melody known only to birds on the wing; it sizzles like a crack of lightning across a pale blue expanse of sky, killing a bird on the wing—or at least a golfer.

Blame is the name; perfection the game. Here's how it is played:

a) Player No. 1 is perfect and, therefore, infallible.

b) Player No. 2 is imperfect and, therefore, fallible.

Rule 1: If a Perfect player makes a mistake, he ceases to be perfect and, furthermore, disappoints his parents.

Rule 2: If the mistake was "not his fault," it doesn't count.

Object of Game:

Player No. 1 attempts to get through life without committing any mistakes by "laying blame" on Player No. 2 whenever a potential mistake occurs. Player No. 2, usually a low achiever and/or younger sibling, has no object whatsoever and is interchangeable as well as quite dispensible. Yes, Player No. 2 may be Player No. 1's spouse.

Strategies

There are a number of interesting strategies which Player No. 1 may employ. Why not try a few of the following?

Blame Strategies That Work

STRATEGY	PERFECT EXAMPLE
1) The "Why didn't you tell me?" maneuver.	"Why didn't you tell me I was running late? You know how I hate clocks."
2) The "You made me" move	"Damn! Now see what you've done? You made me mess up again. Now please be quiet!"

3) The "Anger switch"	"You made me so mad I couldn't help myself and said all kinds of horrible things to you and put you down for eating quiche . . ."
4) The "Bad luck" gambit	"If I could just get a break . . . but with my luck, it would probably be my neck."
5) The "Inanimate object" objection	"How can he expect me to do quality work with an outdated typewriter like this? Well, if he wants errors, he'll get errors."
6) "Bad genes"	"If I were seven feet tall, I'd be playing center for the Lakers too."
7) "If I had only known"	"If I had only known it was your birthday, I would have found you a perfect gift (or at least a cheap card)."
8) "Environmental handicap"	"When you think about it, a 'D' is pretty good when you consider that during my early, formative years I was conditioned by my subculture to avoid studying in favor of drugs, sex, and rock 'n' roll.

9) The "Prejudice trump"	"The only reason I didn't get the job was that they needed a Black woman of Oriental ancestry who speaks Spanish."
10) The "Parental shift"	"What do you expect from me? My father was an alcoholic."
11) The "Self-effacing" ploy	"What do you expect from me? I'm an alcoholic."
12) The "Direct charge"	"What do you expect from me? I'm living with an alcoholic."
13) "The Sibling slip"	*Mother:* "Who left the top off the ketchup bottle?" *You:* "Lisa did it." *Mother:* "But Lisa left home five years ago." *You:* "Lisa *still* did it."

Perfect Technique No. 5:

"Justify" (Formerly "Rationalize")

Whether or not you've transformed your jargon to accommodate the new-wave, upbeat version of that old familiar Freudian standby, "rationalization," I can't recommend this perfect technique highly enough. As my old training psychotherapist used to say, "Mikey, rationalize and the whole world rationalizes with you, but cry and you'll cry on the psychiatric unit at Pino Community Hospital with twenty other inpatients who drool a lot, and four times a day a fat woman wearing white will drug you with antidepressants so that your mouth gets dry, your eyes twitch, and you pee green."

OK. So Babe tended to exaggerate a little, but his basic point is well taken. Once you've mastered the flimsy art of Justification, you will be surprised how much support you will get from people.

For example: You've arrived late for the Bridge Club. You could take responsibility by saying,

"Gee, guys, I'm sorry. I just blew it. I promise to allow more time next week."

Of course, you may just as well slit your wrists and bleed to death as far as jeopardizing your perfection is concerned. So why not try a little justification and say,

"Gee, guys, I can't believe how bad the traffic was; but I look at it this way, if I were always on time, you would get so bored with me."

Them:

"Oh, don't worry about it. Besides it gave us time to discuss the Halloween Bazaar. By the way, did you bring the list of companies that we want to invite?"

You:

"Oh, the list . . . well . . . uh . . . you know, I've been thinking. Is it really wise to make this thing so commercial? I thought we should discuss it."

Them:

"Good idea, Steve, but let's ask our wives. They're so good when it comes to business things. You were smart to wait."

Now wasn't that better? And though Justification does require more thinking than Blame or Lying, I'm sure that with a little practice you'll be twisting facts with the best of them (the "best of them," by the way, are overprotective mothers justifying their child's misbehavior to second grade teachers.)

What Is Justification?

Let's look at it this way: What *is* a mistake? Really. There are no absolute authorities on what qualifies as a mistake, no international tribunal to hand down decisions. . . .

Judge: "In the case of The Planet Earth vs. Frederick Esposito, the People's Perfect Court No. 196 hereby declares that Mr. Esposito did, in fact, commit a heinous mistake when he rudely hung up on his daughter's ex-boyfriend without first checking to learn the purpose of the call, which we determine would have led his daughter to a promising position as a missionary in Borneo. For his mistake, Mr. Esposito is hereby eliminated from the rolls of the Perfect. A note will, of course, be sent home to his parents."

Well, it would be nice if we had such a procedure (of course, it would be nice if we had procedures for repairing Italian sports cars, too), but why not turn this quirk of judicial oversight to your advantage? Since there is no absolute authority as to what is a mistake and what isn't, why not make the decision yourself? Of course, you'll want to be fair, so when you commit something that resembles a mistake, you'll need a good explanation.

This "good explanation" is the heart of Justification, and can be broken down into three categories which, when properly mastered, offer you a defense system that will have Pentagon Generals and Freudian Analysts beating a path to your door.

1) "I had a good reason."
2) "Bad grass."
3) "Sweet inflation."

Let's take a closer look at "Bad grass" as an example of these Justification techniques.

Bad Grass

This technique is admittedly stolen from Sigmund Freud who admittedly stole it from Aesop, formerly with Aesop's Fables, Inc. Aesop, you may recall, wrote a story about a fox who became frustrated and potentially quite depressed when he was unable to reach some grapes which he desired. Rather than suffer the indignities of failure, the fox muttered something about the grapes probably being sour anyway, and scurried off to his psychotherapist.

Unbeknown to Aesop, a rock 'n' roll drummer with a Ph.D. in Urban Planning and a $200 pair of hand-stitched cowboy boots had a similar experience years later in a cow pasture in north Georgia. While waiting for his contact to arrive, this young entrepeneur fantasized lazily about the gorgeous green crop of marijuana that awaited him—how delicious it would taste and the money it would bring! As he was happily daydreaming, two Federal marshals came up from behind, spit chewing tobacco on his boots and placed him under arrest.

As he was being hauled away, an adolescent fox in

"If you don't get what you want, don't want
what you don't get."

search of wild grapes was surprised to hear him mutter under his bad breath, "Oh, well . . . it was probably 'bad grass' anyway."

The moral of both these stories is: "If you don't get what you want, don't want what you don't get." And the easiest way of doing that is to make it bad. After all, Perfect people *always* get what they want, don't they? So, if you're going to be perfect, then you have to assume that if you didn't get it, then you must not really have wanted it; and, besides, it was "bad grass" anyway.

For example:

1) **Situation:** Your fiancee breaks off the engagement by inserting her engagement ring in the ear of a Tom Turkey and leaving it in your refrigerator.

    Justification: "What an immature thing to do. Doesn't she know how much turkeys cost? Good riddance."

2) **Situation:** After six months of interviewing for a plum job, they have narrowed it down to you and a woman who looks suspiciously like an aging Miss Piggy. During the final interview, you let it slip that you once did time for making obscene phone calls to your mother-in-law, and Miss Piggy gets the job.

    Justification: First, talk to everyone you can find who ever worked for the sleazy company. Ask them what they thought of the place, *but only listen to the negative part* (by now you should be skilled at filtering out unwanted information). List these negative remarks on a large piece of poster board and tape it to the mirror that hangs over your water bed. Every night before you go to sleep, say smugly to yourself, "Whew . . . that was close; thank God for pigs." If you don't feel better in a week, rent a villa in the Caribbean and repeat the procedure there. For some reason, all the Perfect techniques work better in a villa in the Caribbean.

The Perfect Person's Favorite Word:

Should

as in:
- You should have reminded me.
- You should have done it by now.
- You should have thought of that sooner.
- You should be more careful, considerate, conscientious . . .

The Perfect Person's Favorite Contraction:

Shouldn't

as in:
- You shouldn't have done it that way.
- You shouldn't speak without thinking.
- You shouldn't make stupid mistakes.*
- You shouldn't be so careless, inconsiderate, lazy . . .

*Are there any other kind?

". . . male rats that have been conditioned to lie are 80% more successful at picking up female rats in simulated singles bars."

Perfect Technique No. 6:

"Lie"

More and more people are waking up to the many benefits of lying. Although a few people still insist on living in the past, these "honesty mongers," as I call them, are fast dwindling.

Research on lying is still sparse, but in addition to the perfect technique that I will discuss with you in a minute, here are some important findings that the scientific journals have overlooked.

1) It has been demonstrated that people who practice the art of lying are less likely to be convicted of mail fraud in New York than those who plead guilty.

2) A longitudinal study in Scandinavia clearly found that children who lied regularly to their teachers earned 40 percent more income when they became adults, at comparable jobs, and were twice as likely to become lawyers.

3) A medical team from Stillmore, Georgia, has disproved the myth that lying makes your nose grow. Unfortunately, it doesn't make your other things grow either.

4) Behavior scientists working with Skinner boxes have found that male rats who have been conditioned to lie are 80 percent more successful at picking up female rats in simulated singles bars.

5) They also found that *men* who have been conditioned to lie are 95 percent more successful at picking up women in real singles bars, and this figure jumps to an incredible 220 percent when the man says that he works for a major record company when he actually sells aluminum siding for a living.

6) Golfers who lie add an average of six shots to their score when they temporarily stop the practice of lying. Unfortunately, there are no long-term follow-up studies on this subject because researchers have been unable to find any golfer willing to give up lying for any significant length of time.

7) Emanuel Wont, a German philosopher now living in Pascagoula, Mississippi, has made several important observations concerning the benefits of lying and marriage. Particularly, he noted that the traditional American marriage ceremony centers around the "Big Question"; that is, "Do you _____ take this _____ to be your lawfully wed-

ded _____ . . . *until death do you part?"* Since the divorce rate is approaching 50 percent, and since everybody is still alive when they divorce, and since 100 percent of the couples married reply, "I do," to the Big Q, Wont reasoned that half of all marriages begin with a Big Lie. He reasoned further that since these people were unhappy in their marriages, it was the Big Lie that enabled them to get out of the marriage, while those who had told the truth, who really meant "till death do us part," were stuck with what might be unhappy marriages and certainly with high mortgage payments. He then gobbled down his milk and animal crackers and went to bed alone, except for Goethe, his stuffed Panda.

8) Anthropologists studying adolescent mating behavior in swamp and grassland habitats report that those teenagers who lie to their parents about what they have been doing while out past curfew, have significantly more fun than those who don't.

Four Rules for Better Lying

As the research suggests, many people have taken up the art of lying with admirable results. Unfortunately, more often than not, the technique backfires and the unfortunate liar winds up apologizing all over himself in a red-faced crescendo of guilt and embarrassment. Sometimes his reputation is so damaged that he becomes unable to find honest work anymore and must resort to a life of politics.

Such a pity. With a few simple rules, lying can be made as simple as, say, distorting the news or projecting economic recoveries:

Rule No. 1: Don't Skimp

In other words, if you're going to lie, lie. Don't tell half lies, white lies, fibs, stories, exaggerations, or half-truths. Take a tip from the boys down at the Third Reich: lie big.

Rule No. 2: Look 'em in the Eye

For some unknown reason, most people still believe that nice, honest people usually look you in the eye when they are trying to be convincing, and therefore, *anybody* who looks you in the eye must also be honest. Don't question the illogic of this practice, just cash in. Or, as they said during the Revolution, "Don't lie until you see the whites of their eyes."

Rule No. 3: Sound Sincere

Simple enough to do, this rule is often overlooked. Your voice is a powerful tool. Train it to work for you, or it will inevitably give you away.

Rule No. 4: Never Admit a Lie

Perfect people simply cannot afford the luxury of admitting a lie. Once a lie is admitted, Perfection dies an ignoble death. Maintain your position at all costs. Yes, even as you descend the stairs of Air Force One for the last time, hounded out of office by the Pathological Turkeys, look the camera right in the eye and in your most sincere voice say it once again, "I am not a crook."

The Strange Case of Richard Nixon

It grieves me to have to write this page, but I believe that someone has to have the courage to expose Richard Nixon, the 35th President of the United States. Very simply stated, it appears that as of this writing, Richard Milhouse Nixon is going soft.

Listen to this. Richard Nixon was the only Perfect President this country ever had. With uncanny precociousness, he mastered the perfect techniques of "Dodge 'em" and "I could if I wanted to" while still a toddler. By age five he was tackling such skills as "Blame" (which later was to become a trademark, such was his virtuosity with the instrument) and "Justification." He virtually invented the modern day use of the "Attack and Distract" techniques, and I understand he could handle sixteen variations of "The Lie" before graduating from Elementary School.

Even when Nixon lost the California gubernatorial race in 1962, he was able to maintain his perfection with an expert delivery of the "Self-Effacing Ploy" when he told newsmen, "You won't have Richard Nixon to kick around anymore."

What a man. What an example of Perfection to hold up for our children to emulate. Through Watergate, the hearings, the incrimination of his closest aides, Nixon used his Perfect skills so well that even stepping down from the Presidency could not be used to un-perfect him.

But something has changed with Nixon. I read the other day that he had admitted lying now and then while in office. Well, of course! How else was he suppose to maintain his perfection (and we Americans do expect perfection from our presidents, don't we)? But *admitting* that he lied is an unforgivable violation of Rule No. 4 for Better Lying, and automatically renders the man (if he *is* still a man) *imperfect*.

Richard Nixon has gone soft. Mothers, tell your children. It begins with telling the truth, but watch, soon he will be accepting responsibility and admitting mistakes.

Before you know it, this one-time giant of a man, this one-time Perfect man, will be reduced to a decent man. Tragic.

Don't let it happen to you.

The Cost of Going Perfect

Going Perfect, like going public, is not without its costs (though legal fees, thank you, are not one of them). Let's just say that your final decision concerning Perfection should be carefully weighed against these few minor, insignificant, hardly-worth-mentioning costs:

1) Because so few people are willing to become Perfect, you will find most human beings hopelessly inferior. You will, therefore, have no friends, and will die lonely and miserable.

2) Though members of the opposite sex will be attracted to your Perfection at first, your lovers will eventually feel intimidated, resentful, and will feel like leaving you—in that order. You will, therefore, have no lasting relationships, and will die lonely and miserable.

3) Your family, once proud of your Perfection will become defensive and testy. One by one they will abandon you. Only your mother will remain loyal. But she will pass away twenty-five years before you. You will therefore have no family, and will die lonely and miserable.

Perfect Test No. 3:

Q. What is the one thing of which Perfect People are secretly afraid?

A. Dying lonely and miserable.

Copping Out

Many people get to this point in the book and begin having second thoughts about Perfection. "Being Perfect is nice," they say, "but I'm not sure *I want* to die lonely and miserable." If *you* find such thoughts creeping into your otherwise Perfect mind, why not try rubbing baboon fat on your head and banging it repeatedly against the walls of the San Diego Zoo. Perhaps one of the attendants will mistake you for a lower primate, and give you a home in the Monkey House where you can live out your life free from all your other obligations as well, and you can continue to waste your potential eating bananas, scratching obscenely in front of little children, and writing self-help books.

Or else you can just bite the bullet of Perfection, and take your immortal place in history. It is yours for the asking. Isn't that worth dying lonely and miserable? It sure beats dying from deep breathing and the other degenerate stress-reduction techniques that are quietly sucking the achievement motive out of your bloodstream. Don't you realize that meditation is no more a substitute for motivation than pickled herring is for lobster tails?

What are you going to do: continue saying mantras, affirmations, and rational self-statements until the Messiah at the Rancho Tropicana Spiritual Awareness and Investment Center has an opening for a new massage student? Is that what you want: a life of vitamins and chiropractic? Are you going to lie down naked like a new age satyr in a hot tub filled with mayonnaise and sex manuals? Are you willing to be prayed over by regression therapists and cultists, and have electrical engineers from Zen Motorcycle repair shops "transform" you into conscious awareness and stupid stuff like that? Do you want them to string you upside down by your inversion boots, and Jazzercize and Fonda you through erratic headphones for hours on end, and force-feed you bean sprouts and Tofu, and take away your inalienable right to nuclear annihilation?

No, of course you don't. You want to be Perfect. And you can, too. Remember, all you have to do is:

- Assert, " I could if I wanted to."
- Dodge 'em
- Blame
- Attack and distract
- Justify
- Lie

. . . and be sure:

- Never attempt anything new.
- Never attempt anything difficult.
- Never take a risk.

- Never attempt to study a foreign language.
- Never admit a mistake.
- Never admit a character flaw.
- Never show negative emotions.
- Never attempt to be modest, demure, humble or in any way unassuming.
- And never, ever ask for your money back.

Willkommen, mein narr, willkommen.

Our Unconditional Guarantee

If for any reason you are dissatisfied with this book, simply return it to the author and he will cheerfully sell it again to someone else.